The Bend in the River

Jacqueline A. Baldwin

Copyright © 2024 Jacqueline A. Baldwin

All rights reserved. No part of this book may be used or reproduced by any means, graphic, electronic, or mechanical, including photocopying, recording, taping, or by any information storage retrieval system without the written permission of the publisher, except in the case of brief quotations embodied in critical articles and reviews.

ISBN Paperback: 978-1-954493-71-1

Front Cover Photo by Jacqueline A. Baldwin

Back Cover Photo by Barbara Swenson Studio

Cover Design by Elizabeth B. Hill

Published by Green Heart Living Press

This is a work of creative nonfiction. The events are portrayed to the best of the author's memory. While all the stories in this book are true, some names and identifying details have been changed to protect the privacy of the people involved. This book is designed to provide information and motivation to our readers. It is sold with the understanding that the publisher is not engaged to render any type of psychological, legal, or any other kind of professional advice. The content is the sole expression and opinion of its author, and not necessarily that of the publisher. No warranties or guarantees are expressed or implied by the publisher's choice to include any of the content in this volume. Neither the publisher nor the author shall be liable for any physical, psychological, emotional, financial, or commercial damages, including, but not limited to, special, incidental, consequential, or other damages. Our views and rights are the same: You are responsible for your own choices, actions, and results.

Contents

Dedication	1
Foreword	3
Prologue	7
1. Where the Journey Begins	13
2. Lighthouse	21
3. Expedition Life	33
4. The Island of If Only	47
5. On the Rocks	55
6. Rough Seas Ahead Cap'n	65
7. Forgiveness	77
8. Fair Winds And Following Seas	85
About the Author	91
About the Illustrator	93

Dedication

Throughout the tumultuous journey called life, my deepening faith has been the rock on which I stand. There have been many times I felt far from God yet I know now He has been by my side the entire time.

The phrase "it takes a village" has never been more true than when it comes to this book! My village is enormous, and I am eternally grateful to be blessed with such an incredible, supportive group of humans.

This book is dedicated to each and every person who is knit into the beautiful tapestry of my life.

I want to specifically give a shout-out to my sons, Sam and Ben. Your unconditional love and your faith in me even when I didn't believe in myself is what has propelled me forward through some of the most difficult days of my life.

You are my greatest encouragers, the best listeners, the ones who have provided strength when I felt too worn out to move on. Words cannot express the love I have for you, both today and forever.

Foreword

In life, we often encounter individuals who, through their words and actions, become beacons of light guiding us through the darkest of times. Jackie is one such person. *The Bend in the River* is not just a memoir, but a profound testament to resilience, patience, and faith. As you embark on this journey alongside Jackie, you'll discover a transformative power within her words—a power that brings healing to the wounded soul and solace to those facing trials and tribulations.

Within the pages of this book, you'll encounter Jackie's life story, a tapestry woven with threads of perseverance, fearlessness, and a deep belief in the power of grace and forgiveness. Her experiences of navigating difficult relationships, embracing the challenges of motherhood, and confronting societal norms will resonate deeply with readers, reminding us all of our own capacity for resilience and growth.

As you read, you'll witness Jackie's unwavering faith in action—a faith that infuses every aspect of her life with kindness, compassion, and loyalty. You'll journey alongside her as she embarks on a solo adventure down the river, finding strength and peace in solitude, and embracing the unknown with courage and determination.

Through Jackie's courageous storytelling, taboo topics such as sexual abuse are brought into the light, empowering readers to break free from the chains of guilt and isolation. Her words offer a beacon of hope to those who have suffered in silence, reminding us all that healing and redemption are possible, even in our darkest moments.

As you read Jackie's story, you'll be inspired to embrace life's challenges with courage and grace, knowing that around every bend in the river lies the promise of hope and healing. May her words fill your heart with joy and hope, and may you find light and inspiration around every river bend.

-Ria Irons

Prologue

Our lives are a perfectly written novel. From the day we are born, all the joy, triumphs, beauty, obstacles, pain, suffering, and even trauma, will lead to the next chapter. Some novels will be clear with progression from one chapter to another. But for many, it may seem very unclear what the next chapter will bring.

For me, my life has been much like my experiences on the Connecticut River. Sometimes harrowing, many times peaceful, but always ever-changing. From the time I was a little girl, I have been drawn to this river that literally splits our small state in half.

My father was a marine transport pilot in the Pacific theater during World War II. He also was a flight instructor, so it was only fitting that he started a flight school, Baldwin Aviation, when I was a young girl. My father and eldest brother, Kevin, as the flight instructors, taught dozens of students to fly. I did not fully appreciate what an incredible experience this was until I was older. The flight school owned and operated four airplanes and for a time we were based at the Goodspeed Airport in East Haddam, Connecticut.

The airport sat along the banks of the winding river. I spent my summers welcoming students as they waited in our makeshift office inside the hangar for their lessons. If there was time during the day my father usually took me up for a quick spin which I cherished.

In my downtime, I would spend hours hanging out down by the river, watching it flow. Sometimes calm and serene, other times rushing and choppy.

One of only two remaining swing bridges on the Connecticut River connects East Haddam with Haddam. As a kid, I was always thrilled to watch as it swung open, allowing for the taller vessels and high-masted sailboats to pass through.

I longed to be on the water. To drift along on the current, and let it take me where it desired. You see, I wanted to escape, to be a different person, to leave behind the deep trauma that permeated every ounce of me. To me the river could wash me clean, take me to a place where I would be beautiful again.

How was I to know the river would be instrumental in my healing decades later? My experiences on the river would become an analogy to my entire life journey and would in fact bring me to be able to relate the perfect novel of my life. God has been preparing me my whole existence for THIS!

I still do not know what lies beyond the bend in the river, but I do know that I have never felt more prepared, paddling in great anticipation to embrace whatever I encounter.

May you find the inner strength that you have been developing all along. May you find flat water where you rest in His peace, so you are prepared for the next rough water where you will say "Bring It!" I am ready because I know that around the bend in the river, I will find calm water like glass again.

Isaiah NLT 41:10

"Don't be afraid, for I am with you. Don't be discouraged, for I am your God. I will strengthen you and help you, I will hold you up with my victorious right hand."

1

WHERE THE JOURNEY BEGINS

Discovering one's self in your fifties is both terrifying and exhilarating. You see, I have spent my entire life with a mask on to disguise an inner self-loathing, a deep insecurity that comes from feeling completely unworthy. That is what becomes of a four-year-old girl who lost her innocence at the hands of her grandfather.

The abuse started after my grandmother passed. My grandfather, my mother's father, moved in with us until my father had completed building an in-law apartment onto our house. The trauma then continued, as I was invited to spend time with him alone in his apartment. He would pay me dimes and quarters to do things that no young girl should do.

I vividly remember the day someone discovered us together in his famous rose garden. They were horrified by what they saw.

As I was running away sobbing, I heard them yelling at my grandfather. This person NEVER raised their voice, so I knew instinctively that this was really bad.

I truly believe no one had any idea of the extent of the abuse.

After a few days, I found myself at my grandfather's apartment again. He resumed the abuse, telling me this was our "special secret." He said not to tell my mother or anyone else, because they would not understand.

Why did I go back? As a young girl, I was raised to respect my elders, to listen and follow, and to do what I was told.

At that age, I had not yet learned discernment and to understand that even elders can make mistakes or do bad things. I did not realize that this directive was not meant to be a blanket carte blanche.

I thought, because he was my grandfather, he would never hurt me.

I began to take on the feelings of shame, guilt, and unworthiness that would define and impact me well into adulthood.

So, for two years this continued, until the day I "killed my grandfather." I was watching Saturday morning cartoons when I heard the banging over the antics of Bugs Bunny and Elmer Fudd. During the commercial, I got up to find out what the banging was and walked outside where my grandfather's apartment was connected to our home. I could see through the storm door that he was on his knees motioning for me to open the door. As I did that he fell out onto me, barely able to speak. With a raspy voice, he managed to get the words out, "Go get your mother." I did as I was told.

The ambulance took him away with my mother following. My brothers tried reassuring me that he was just going to get some rest for a few days.

Later, when I was told he died, I was sad yet oddly relieved. I had wanted the "visits" to end. But then terror overtook my emotions, because I felt I had killed my grandfather by not going out when I first heard the banging!

I had prayed to not be tormented any longer. Had I made my grandfather die? I convinced myself I had! My mother would surely hate me forever for killing her father! I now had TWO ugly secrets that I must keep hidden.

It was then that I completely disassociated myself from that little girl. It was the only way I would survive. This trauma was to permeate every aspect of my life into adulthood.

I know this is a heavy way to begin this book, but please bear with me. I promise that there is a glorious outcome. A "rise from the ashes" victory! I share this not to garner sympathy or for shock value. I share this story to bring hope and healing. I have discovered that through faith I have been made resilient, bold, incredibly strong, fiercely loyal, and humble.

My mourning has been turned into dancing!

As a fully known and loved daughter of God I am called to come alongside those who may feel "less than," unqualified, unworthy, perhaps even filled with shame, as I had been.

I have to admit that sharing my journey, which was filled with less-than-perfect moments, is uncomfortable, to say the least. However, I must share the time spent in the depths of the valley in order for you to see how grace has lifted me to the highest mountaintop and made me brand new.

This journey has not been an easy one. As a matter of fact, there have been times it has been excruciatingly painful. Over the past seven years, my travels took me through confrontation, acknowledgment, grief, forgiveness, healing, discovery, and at long last, the complete inner peace that I have longed for since I was that little girl. I have garnered much knowledge along the way that I wish to share with you.

At the root of my prompting to write this book is my God-given purpose to encourage those who have been wounded, and beckon them to take their own first step toward victory. My desire is for everyone to see themselves as the beautiful person they are. Life's saboteurs can get a hold of us whispering lies into our ear. I imagine that if you have gotten this far, there is something that has resonated with you. Perhaps you are wondering if you are ready to turn the page.

My dear, you DESERVE to feel loved, worthy, and stunningly beautiful, but this must start with YOU. You must first see yourself as priceless, worthy, enough! Only then will you truly believe that others already see you this way. Are you wearing a mask as

I had been? If so, are you ready to shed the mask and let your light pour forth for the entire world to behold? If the answer is yes, then let's step forward together.

2 Corinthians 1:4 NLT

"He comforts us in all our troubles so that we can comfort others. When they are troubled, we will be able to give them the same comfort God has given us."

2
LIGHTHOUSE

Life is messy! It never goes quite the way we envision it in our dreams. Just as I have experienced while paddling my kayak on the river, there may be debris blocking our way, unexpected winds can blow us off course, and treacherous weather that makes navigating challenging at best.

One late fall afternoon I took my kayak out. What was to be a short peaceful paddle to end a Saturday, turned into a harrowing, unexpected life lesson. In early October, the Connecticut River Valley is an explosion of colors as the leaves on the trees put on a vibrant display to behold. Looking at the mosaic of spikes of color across a far-off hillside always reminds me of the Magic Rocks my brothers and I used to grow in glass bowls when we were kids.

I had finished hosting a full-day financial workshop and desired to unwind a bit on one of the last few warm days that I could get out on the river. I hurried home, quickly changed into a light shirt and shorts, and picked up Baxter, my yellow Labrador Retriever and trusted companion. It looked like we could still catch the last couple of hours of daylight.

We drove quickly down to our favorite local launch site on the Coginchaug River, which leads into the Mattabesett River and then out to the Connecticut River. We had taken this short paddle many times before. The peacefulness of the smaller tributaries brings a sense of calm. This is where I take time to refill my proverbial cup so that I may continue to pour out to others.

As I paddled toward the Connecticut River, I could hear the bustle of the cars crossing over State Highway 9. Soon I could begin to hear the roar of motor boats on the much larger river. I enjoyed venturing out from the peaceful coziness for a brief stimulating encounter with the longest New England river, which runs from Canada down to Long Island Sound, before returning to the serenity of my hometown waterway.

This is a very familiar jaunt, which caused me to be a bit cavalier and forget all the safety measures and planning that one should take every time entering the water. When I took my inflatable kayak (yes, I said inflatable) out from my trunk where it lives all summer long for just such impromptu trips, I realized I did not have my PFD (personal floatation device) with me. I had Baxter's, and like any good dog mom, that was what was important. After all, this was to be just a short paddle.

I decided I would forgo going out on the big river and just go to the mouth before turning back. I would be okay, I rationalized. I also realized that in my haste I had forgotten to pack a water bottle! Oh well, it wasn't that warm, so hydration wouldn't be quite as big a deal. I had no towel to dry Baxter off. I had no snacks. I didn't have much.

Now that little voice in my head started saying, "Jackie, perhaps you should just call it a day and not go out." I could hear my father's voice, a former Marine transport pilot in World War II and flight instructor saying, "You should always have a safety checklist that you go through each and every time to avoid situations such as these." And yet I talked him down, convincing myself that I knew best and that just this once everything would be just fine.

You see, my desire to have what I wanted right then and there pushed aside any common sense that was trying to delay my immediate pleasure.

So, we set out, paddling along and soaking in the tranquility of the late fall. The sun was warm, and the smell of autumn leaves wafted through my nostrils. My body released the stresses of the day, and all was peaceful and right in the world!

After about an hour on the water, I had only seen a couple of other kayakers heading back toward the launch. I saw one motorized fishing boat. Observing the sun sliding down toward the horizon, I decided to turn around and head back to the launch site.

I suddenly realized that I had also forgotten my sunglasses. The sun was low, at eye level, blinding me. I squinted as much as I could while still being able to see. Tears were streaming down my cheeks, making it nearly impossible to see ahead with the sun glistening off of the still water. The reeds had grown over the summer, obscuring the confluences. I soon realized I must have missed my turn. The sun was dropping rapidly and the chill of the air was settling in. Darkness would be upon me in about 20 minutes. I had to find the entrance to the Coginchaug.

What should have been strikingly familiar now was unrecognizable. An uneasy feeling was beginning to sink into the pit of my stomach.

The fishing boat I had seen earlier now had its headlight on as it returned to the dock on the Connecticut River. My pride would not allow me to yell out for help. I watched them as they motored further away and then out of sight.

Baxter and I were the only ones left out there now. I began feeling desperately alone. The sun had completely set, and darkness was coming fast. I was cold and hungry, and fear was clouding my mind.

I heard the flapping of wings of very large birds; they may as well have been pterodactyls that would pluck us from the boat to go and feed their babies. Your mind does strange things when you are panicking!

I calmed myself, remembering it was just the great blue herons settling in for the night. I checked my phone; the battery was down to 5%. Oh great, I hadn't planned that very well either!

Baxter came to the back of the boat to be closer to me, sensing an anxiety attack coming on. I began thinking we could try to get to the river bank and put the kayak over us to stay warm and wait until the sun came up in the morning, but I realized that was not a realistic solution. My arms were aching now as I was paddling faster and harder, desperately trying to find my way in the dark. Nothing looked familiar, my head was swimming, and my breath was short. Surely, I was going to pass out. There wasn't even moonlight to show me the way.

At last, I had almost given up! I stopped paddling in defeat. Tears poured down my face, and the lump in my throat constricted my ability to swallow. I was feeling hopeless and foolish for being so careless.

I could see it now: "Mid-fifty-year-old woman and her dog last seen paddling the river by a local fisherman now reported missing. News at 11!" I was going to be the story that people listen to and shake their heads, commenting, "What was she thinking?"

We all have watched stories like this on the news or social media. I have read the responses by the uninformed commentators, calling out the seemingly ridiculous actions of the subjects of the story. I can say this because I am embarrassed to admit that I used to be among the scoffers. I may not have been so bold as to type it out and hit "Post" but I certainly had uncharitable thoughts. As if I would have known better than to do...fill in the blank with whatever was done.

I talked myself down and remembered I had other senses beyond sight. I strained to listen to hear the direction the din of cars was coming from. I needed to paddle toward that noise. This was what was going to take me out to the Connecticut River where I could paddle downriver to the harbor boat dock. I decided to use what precious battery I had left to text my friend that I was okay, but could he please come to pick me up at the dock? I gained courage; we were going to make it home tonight!

I estimated I had about another forty minutes of paddling steady to get there. I paddled faster as I heard the welcome sound of rushing cars getting louder. I knew that when I smelled the diesel from the train bridge I was getting close to breaking out into the main river. Yes! We had made it onto the mighty Great River! The Arrigoni Bridge came into view, lit up in all its glory. That bridge had never looked more beautiful to me.

I had now been on the water for nearly four hours. The temperature was dropping like a rock. I had used up all my energy and my muscles were in need of food. But we were going to make it. Just another twenty minutes or so.

As silly as this sounds, I wanted to look calm, cool, and collected as I paddled past the partiers at the outdoor bar overlooking the river. Pride wouldn't allow me to be seen as less than a stoic, confident woman that I was far from feeling on the inside. Everyone stopped and began yelling out, "Hey, look at that crazy lady with her dog out there at this time of night!" Yup! That's me, the crazy lady!

As I approached the dock, my arms were feeling like they were going to fall off. My adrenaline had been coursing through my body, propelling me forward. Now, knowing that I was almost there, it finally let up, leaving me insufferably drained. I had not eaten in over eleven hours, and I was now dehydrated.

I saw a light moving back and forth on the dock. My friend was there, shining his light like a lighthouse guiding me in. Baxter saw him at the same time and jumped overboard to swim the last 25 feet in. I got to the dock, and my friend grabbed my hand and pulled me out of the kayak onto the bobbing dock. My legs felt like rubber and my body immediately started shaking, partly from the cold and partly from sheer exhaustion, both mentally and physically.

I began to sob. I had been so foolish and taken so many risks. How very ridiculous I had been. My internal judge was rebuking me and making me feel small. Shame piled on as I heard the voices of those from my past who made me believe I was going to fail at whatever I was endeavoring to do. I wasn't capable, smart enough, or strong enough to accomplish anything beyond what were safe, in-the-box aspirations.

As we drove in silence to where I had left my car, I reflected on this harrowing journey. I could have let old lies cause me to sink into a place of regret and let the fear of what could have been prevent me from ever attempting such a trip again.

Instead, I was reminded that *"we know that in all things God works for the good of those who love him, who have been called according to his purpose"* (Romans 8:28 NIV).

I began viewing this experience as a blessing; a life lesson. My desire for immediate gratification had caused me to ignore the flashing red lights trying to warn me of danger ahead. This could have resulted in a disastrous outcome, not only for me, but for Baxter, who trusts me implicitly.

I should have paused to consider the consequences of not being prepared.

I needed to be sure I had the proper safety equipment and provisions. I should have had a backup plan, including letting someone know where I was going and what time I expected to return, so they would have known when and where to begin looking for me. I should have considered the remaining daylight and shortened the trip. The list goes on!

At the same time, this adventure proved to me that I AM stronger than I realized. I HAVE the capacity and fortitude to dig deep inside rather than giving in to fear. Casting fear aside is what was necessary if I was to find the answers. And lastly, I learned not to be too proud or feel so alone that I don't reach out for support. God has put people in my life for just that purpose. And God himself desires for us to call out from the darkness and come live in the light knowing we are never alone. Perhaps this recollection in my life has encouraged you to call out in times of loneliness, fear or desperation and know there is a lighthouse that will be there to keep you from crashing into the rocks and will guide you safely home.

John 1:5 NLT

"The light shines in the darkness, and the darkness can never extinguish it."

3

EXPEDITION LIFE

I have gotten it in my head that I am going to segment-paddle the entire 410 miles of the Connecticut River, source to sea. My goal had been to paddle every mile of this glorious river that I have longed to be on since I was that little girl by the end of 2022.

As is prone to happen, life had some detours, so here I am, in 2024, with no less resolve to complete this expedition. As I write this, I have nearly 200 miles left to complete my goal.

I can hear you asking, "Girl, what made you decide to do that?"

I wish I had a tremendously inspirational answer, but honestly, I don't. I feel like Forrest Gump in the 1994 movie of the same name with Tom Hanks as the lead character. When asked why he decided to run across the country, his response was, "That day, for no particular reason, I decided to go for a little run. So I ran to the end of the road. And when I got there, I thought maybe I'd run to the end of the town. And when I got there, I thought maybe I'd just run across

Greenbow County...For no particular reason, I just kept on going. I just felt like running."

I began segment-paddling the Connecticut portion of the river on a whim. When I first found myself single following the crushing demise of my 25-year marriage, I was seeking ways to get "away" from the world. I would escape by hiking for miles with my best friend, Baxter, exploring new trails and revisiting tried and true ones.

While it was peaceful amid the solitude of the woods, my mind kept wandering back to childhood memories of the ever-flowing water of the river.

At that time, I also was counting every penny. I was completely starting over financially, at ground zero. Not only was I now single with my youngest son still living with me, I felt called to strike out on my own, building my own independent financial advising practice. Let's just say I decided I was going to go big or go home! Sounds a bit crazy? Perhaps!

I knew being on the water always brought me peace, which I desperately was craving. I began researching kayaks that would allow Baxter to join me, would be easy for me to manage by myself, and were affordable. I discovered Sea Eagle inflatable kayaks. At that time, it was a big expense for me at nearly $400! I agonized over spending the money. I kept thinking of all the other things I needed much more than a kayak.

I finally rationalized it by looking at my budget and counting this as my "entertainment" line item for the next several months! Let me tell you, it has more than paid for itself in the incredible experiences I have had and the deep healing that has been brought to my soul.

Now that I am in a better place financially, I often scroll through the new Sea Eagle models, pondering whether I should get a more streamlined version. Each time, I recommit myself to completing this journey with my tried-and-true original kayak. We will finish this journey together!

When I first got the kayak, I did several trial paddles on calm ponds, then graduated to larger lakes and on to small waterways.

Eventually, I felt confident enough to set out on the Connecticut River.

I wanted to actually go somewhere, to have a destination rather than just paddling around and coming back to where I began. At first, it was 10 miles. Then 15 miles.

After experiencing a growing sense of self-confidence and inner peace following each time I took to the water, I began to dream of accomplishing a goal that would stretch me—something that would test my courage, strength, and perseverance.

The expectation throughout our lives is to set goals. While I agree we should set goals I do believe we need to perhaps understand the definition of the word GOAL in order to have the proper expectations. According to the *Merriam-Webster Dictionary*, a goal is "the end **toward** which effort is directed."

Nothing in this definition says anything about attainment. It is all about the intention. It is when GOAL is used in conjunction with other words, such as ATTAINED or ACCOMPLISHED, that it indicates the end was reached.

This puts my mind at peace. While I have every intention of completing this goal, I am going to embrace the adventure along the way. Throughout my life I think I have been so focused on what goals others have achieved that I have robbed myself of soaking in the lessons learned, the scenery that is daily living, and the appreciation for where I am today.

I have been looking at my life all wrong to date. Instead of failure, I have gained wisdom. Rather than looking at myself as a victim, I am a victor. In lieu of feeling as though I have wasted all these years by living anxiously and fearfully, I am choosing to look at this time as being in training for my destined purpose. I can hear my father's voice, saying "That's my girl!"

My father always pushed the envelope and challenged himself. One such journey was his epic trip from Hebron, Connecticut to Disney World, Florida in 31 days by bicycle after triple bypass heart surgery at the age of 64. He had researched, planned, and set a GOAL!

He taught me that you can accomplish anything you desire. Don't ever let anyone tell you it can't be done or that you will fail trying. There is always a way, even if it isn't exactly how you originally envisioned it. While of course it is important to seek and take heed of solid counsel, do not allow negative voices to dissuade you from pursuing your passion.

I spent decades in relationships that were not supportive, which sought to squelch my independence and pursuit of personal growth. Keep close to those who believe in you, provide thoughtful input for consideration, and help talk through decisions to be made.

My mother was always my father's biggest cheerleader and partner. My father embraced adventure his entire life—always choosing the path less traveled (or blazing his own trail). Some may even call some of his endeavors dangerous. The difference was that he was not reckless. He never did anything in haste. It was always thought out, identifying the risks, eliminating the risks he could, and having a contingency plan for those he couldn't.

This bicycle trip was just one such example. Keep in mind that this trip was done before cell phones, GPS, and Amazon. I remember the piles of maps spread out on the dining room table. My father spent hours researching routes, planning where he could resupply, and having shipments delivered, as the weight he carried was a major concern.

He would stop every five days in a hotel to shower, pick up supplies, and get a decent night's sleep. He had contingency plans for equipment malfunction or physical ailments. He had marked on his maps every hospital along the way. He would have daily phone check-ins with my mother from payphones.

I remember the day he left, waving goodbye. This was an adventure riddled with potential danger, yet I knew he would accomplish his goal. My mother and I would next see him a month from then, welcoming him as he pedaled into Walt Disney World over 1,300 miles later.

I could never have imagined then that I would be planning my own adventure 40 years later. Hours of research, studying maps, creating checklists for gear, creating contingency plans. Unlike my father, I have the benefits of a cell phone, GPS, and internet connection while on the water.

The basics of planning such a journey are the same. Identifying risks, eliminating as many as possible, and creating contingency plans for those I can't. I rely heavily on the experiences of other paddlers who have made this journey before me. In fact, there is an entire website dedicated to supporting paddlers in their quest to do the very same thing. I also consult books written by segment paddlers with warnings and tips (some of which I discounted out of my stubbornness thinking I knew better—NOT!) These paddlers also share the rich history and sights of the river to take in along the way.

As I planned, I realized that this was taking on a very spiritual and healing role. As I envision myself paddling, I can see my superhero cape flying in the wind behind me. I see my awkwardness and the trepidation of my early paddles falling off into the water and drifting away in the current of the river, never to be seen again.

I have begun to realize that while the quest is to paddle the 410 miles, the true journey is one of healing my spirit one layer at a time, letting go of my limiting fears, kicking the saboteurs out of my "boat" one at a time.

Another great nugget of wisdom from Forrest Gump is, "My mama always said, 'You've got to put the past behind you before you can move on.'" It is so simplistic in nature, but enormously difficult in the actual "doing."

I have discovered that I used to look in the rearview mirror with eyes that only saw regret, pain, suffering, and lack. This caused me to then pull the car over and stare into my past, becoming immobilized and ineffective. I was stuck on the side of the road, broken down, as the other vehicles passed by me, shaking my car with the wind they created. I wondered where they were going and why I could not seem to get my car back into gear.

Instead, I continued to look back at where I had come from saying to myself, "It wasn't all THAT bad, was it?" Maybe I should just go back to what I know. At least I'd known what I was getting back into. What lies ahead could be worse, right?

I was letting fear of the unknown before me allow me to accept what was critically wounding me from behind.

What I needed to do was to set my sights on what was around the bend in the river. As unnerving as the unknown can be, I am learning to give a big old bear hug to each new experience, no matter how good or challenging. Knowing that, as long as I keep moving toward the goal, I can take as long as I need to in order to achieve the goal.

That being said, by putting it out into the world that I am going to complete this quest, I am now seeking accountability to get 'er done. I also have an even bigger incentive to complete this goal SOON.

I began this journey with my faithful companion Baxter, who is now 10 years old and an 8-year cancer survivor. I cannot imagine paddling the last mile without him at the helm, steadfast and loyal.

Lulu, the spunky and sometimes sassy Havanese, came to our family a few years ago after my dear friend Carmela passed away. Lulu was a city girl who had not had much in the way of outdoor experiences. Carmela's family was not in position to take her in, so I gladly adopted her on one condition: that she adapted well to our family's outdoor lifestyle.

Lulu and I arrived home from the funeral. After having made her acquaintance with Baxter, we all went for our first walk together. All went well! The next step was to go hiking and see how she did off her leash. She did fantastic. Lulu tagged along with Baxter, who always is in the lead, or stayed right by my side. Okay little girl, time to go get your very own PFD and see how you do on the water. Suffice it to say, she took to the kayak like a pro.

Once she got her sea legs, she freely walked about the kayak with ease. Lulu is my friend Carmela in dog form! Carmela was small in stature but had an enormous personality! She had a heart of gold with a wry sense of humor and a big bark when necessary. Sharing this journey with Baxter and Lulu has brought me joy words simply cannot express.

The next crucial piece to accomplishing this goal has been to surround myself with the best accountability partners! I need to have coaches who are there to spur me on and not let me quit. I need cheerleaders who believe that anything can be done if you put your mind to it. I want go-getters in my life that encourage me to be the best version of myself. I have set about recruiting the A-Team!

Anyone who is a naysayer—a person who says "that is impossible," who tells me I should take the path that is well-worn, that it is too dangerous to venture off the road less or never traveled—is ushered to the side.

Author Mark Twain's words come to mind, "Keep away from people who try to belittle your ambitions. Small people always do that, but the really great ones make you feel that you, too, can become great."

I understand my quest will not be easy and at times it will be downright brutal, and I'll make mistakes along the way. It has already proven that to me. I am gaining experience each time I take to the water and learning from my mistakes, and believe me, there have and will continue to be many. But that is the best part! I will never have all the answers; how boring would that be?

I recognize now that navigating through my life's most difficult times, I have acquired wisdom that could never have been taught, inner strength that only comes from being tempered by the fire, and flexibility that comes from being stretched well beyond what I ever thought possible. This has all created a confidence within me that allows me to greet the next trial that life has to offer with courage and determination. These are the gems of life that lead to finding joy in the midst of chaos.

Let me share with you where I have been so far: the vulnerabilities, the missteps, the all-out terrifying moments that have led to the breaking free, the power gained, the sense of inner peace and contentment of who I am today, and the anticipation of what I am yet to become.

God is still writing my story. He knows every step I will take, remaining by my side for each and every one. This understanding has provided a peace beyond anything the world can provide. I only need to stay focused on today. He has got all my tomorrows in His hands.

You have dreams and gifts. Perhaps they are not yet clear. You may have chosen to follow the path less traveled. Don't let anyone tell you not to follow the dream that will manifest your gift. It will be hard at times. At the end of the day, however, you will know you are on the right path when you can FEEL it deep in your soul.

When you know you are doing what God has created you for, you won't allow yourself to give up on it. Discover your gift, my dear one. Don't let fear of failure hold you back. You must move even when it feels like you aren't clear on the direction.

James 1:2-4 NIV

"Consider it pure joy, my brothers and sisters, whenever you face trials of many kinds, because you know that the testing of your faith produces perseverance. Let perseverance finish its work so that you may be mature and complete, not lacking anything."

4
THE ISLAND OF IF ONLY

If only I had more financial security, then I would be truly happy. If only my health were better. If only I looked like I did thirty years ago. If only I had not wasted all those years in unhealthy relationships. If only...fill in your own blank! I had taken up permanent residency on the island of "If Only..."

This was not a tropical island with palm trees swaying on beaches with the lulling sounds of gentle waves lapping up on shore. Oh no! This was a desolate island that was bleak—there was nothing relaxing about it! The land was harsh, with jagged rocks that kept me off balance. The food was edible but lacked flavor. There was no beauty to be seen from my vantage point. The waves would crash against the rocks, splashing me with sobering cold water.

I kept thinking that I was stuck here on the island of "If Only..." until someone would come rescue me.

From time to time, I could hear the sound of soul-filling music and laughter. I could smell the occasional sweet smell of what I imagined must be exquisite flowers wafting in the air. I wondered where it was coming from. How could I find it? I used to look at friends and family, seeing an ease about them, and wonder what that must feel like. It seemed as though they were never rattled. That in spite of the trials they have gone through, they were at peace.

I, on the other hand, lived in constant fight or flight mode. It was exhausting and paralyzing. This led me to make enormously horrible decisions throughout my life which just deepened my self-shame.

How many times in life do we make choices that in hindsight we beat ourselves up over, feeling stupid or worse? I am here to tell you that EVERYTHING can bring you wisdom, courage and strength. It is not that you are saying "Hooray, I am so glad I went through that painful/scary/awful event." Goodness knows, none of us are overjoyed to have had the negative events in our lives. But we can decide what effect these experiences will have on our lives going forward.

I am a work in progress, as I imagine everyone is. I am learning to reflect on even the darkest moments of my life and pull the wisdom and the gifts that I take away from those times, and employ them in my life today.

One such example of this is my ability to imagine far outside the box to create opportunities for my family, friends, community, and clients.

This vast imagination was born out of necessity when I was a young girl. My survival technique was to escape my current situation and create another imaginary world where I was safe and loved.

I used to pretend I was living in a far-off glorious place with nothing but laughter and sunshine. I was beautiful, with no hidden, dark, ugly secrets. I imagined myself as a singer on stage, sharing lyrics of love and bringing joy to everyone who was in the audience.

The brilliant Albert Einstein was quoted saying, "Imagination is everything, it is a preview of coming attractions." Truth!

I have spent the past several years facing these ugly events in my life and peeling back the layers of the onion one at a time as I was emotionally able to. This is not something that I just willed away. It has taken lots of work: talk therapy, eye movement desensitization and reprocessing (EMDR) therapy, working with a life coach, prayer, and studying the Word.

The final layer of the healing has been to take the good that has come from each event and leave the ugly behind. This has allowed me to forgive and reflect with grace not only those in my life who I previously felt bitterness toward but myself as well.

By eliminating the root of bitterness from my spirit, I have become more earnestly compassionate. I discovered that I must forgive those who have wounded me so deeply. Otherwise, these wounds will fester and continue to infect my entire being. Perhaps you have found this to be true as well.

The most difficult part was to forgive myself. I believe that took the most work. I grant myself space to make mistakes now and put them in proper context in order to take away the wisdom for future reference.

The actor Denzel Washington, during his commencement speech at the University of Pennsylvania, said: "I'm sure...people have told you to make sure you have something to fall back on. 'Make sure you have something to fall back on, honey!' But I've never understood that concept. Don't be afraid to fail, because you WILL fail. If I'm going to fall, I don't want to fall back on anything except my faith. I want to fall forward. I figure that at least this way, I will see what I'm going to hit."

Guess what? This has allowed me to at long last discover where the beautiful music is coming from. I not only can smell the exquisite flowers, but I sit among them and their fields filled with a glorious explosion of color.

I finally got it! The peace that I have seen in others all these years now resides in me. I did it by living right here, right now, and embracing each moment, not waiting to find the blessing sometime way down the road, but grabbing hold of it at this very moment. By doing this, I am able to rid myself of the paralyzing anxiety that used to rob me of joy.

My mother's words of wisdom come to mind here. "Everything will work out for the best, my dear. You may not be able to see it today, but one day you will discover the reason for this season." Oh, how I miss her encouraging nuggets!

Does it mean I am never sad? Of course not, but rather than taking up residence on the "If Only..."

island, I only visit it, taking time to grieve, weep, be upset or even angry, and then paddle back toward the island of beautiful music and exquisite flowers.

Matthew 6:27, 34 NIV

"Can any one of you by worrying add a single hour to your life? Therefore do not worry about tomorrow, for tomorrow will worry about itself. Each day has enough trouble of its own."

5

ON THE ROCKS

I was exhausted and began to wonder what in the world I was doing. What made me think THIS was a good idea? Taking two dogs out for our first overnight kayaking trip in a section of river I had never been on nor even truly researched.

Just the day before, I was packing my gear, checking my list, reviewing the maps again, and making final adjustments. I felt confident. In addition to the books for paddlers of the Connecticut River, I joined a Connecticut River Paddlers online club, and I myself have camping experience as a former Boy Scout leader. Plus, my father taught me so much about hiking and outdoorsmanship. I had established contingency plans, including alternate camping and take-out points.

I sent my entire route to my Land Team (my sons and "Sister from a different Mister") in the event I needed help. The two-day trip was locked in! But a severe storm had come through Connecticut and Massachusetts just a couple of days before, decimating the area and causing widespread power outages from downed trees.

A friend reached out the night before I was to leave, asking if I was still planning on going. She notified me that there had been a sewage spill that was contaminating the entire section of river I had extensively researched and planned to be on. Instead of postponing the trip, I quickly pulled out my books and maps and selected a new 35-mile section to complete. After all, what difference would it make? This section would have to be done at some point anyway.

But I neglected to spend the time researching the new area I'd just chosen. I know! I can hear your thoughts as you are reading this. "Did you not learn anything from your near disastrous night with the pterodactyls?!" Apparently not! It appears that some lessons need to be taught multiple times.

I quickly sent a new makeshift plan to my land crew. After an admittedly restless sleep, off we went that bright Saturday morning. My son and his girlfriend met us at a marina in Massachusetts, which would be our take-out location Sunday night. I would leave my car there. We transferred all the gear into my son's car. He would drive me, Baxter, and Lulu north to our new launch site.

The day started later than I had planned, leaving me feeling a bit harried. In my haste, I left my water shoes in my car back at the marina, now nearly an hour away.

My 85-pound Lab was sitting on my lap because all the gear ended up IN the car because there was no room in the trunk. As we drove, I read up on the section of the river I had chosen the night before.

The authors of the book for paddlers were very detailed about each segment of the river. It seemed like just what the doctor had ordered. I needed this little getaway. The COVID-19 pandemic had disrupted every aspect of my life, and this time to get back into nature would be restorative.

As I was quickly skimming the author's description of this new segment, I got to the part where they were warning of motorized watercraft. I discounted their concern as I was used to the motor boats in Middletown.

Remember how I ignored flashing red lights before? Guess who did that again?

We arrived at the launch point just before 11 a.m. It was going to be tight, but I thought we ought to make it to our camping spot before sundown. I inflated the kayak, and after a few other missteps, the dogs and I were off.

Waving goodbye and turning to paddle down the Deerfield River to connect with the Connecticut River, I felt a bit unsettled from the change of plans. With both dogs assuming their positions—Lulu behind me in the stern and Baxter as my lookout at the bow—I began to settle into an easy rhythm. Hearing the paddles in the water moving us forward, watching the egrets perched on a log, and sunbathing turtles plopping into the water as we approached, all the peace of being on the river began to fill my spirit.

It had been an unusually dry summer, and the water levels were low. This was when I really missed my water shoes! I had to get out and walk the kayak, which is about 350 pounds with all of us and the gear. Baxter was thrilled to be able to get out and walk and play in the shallow river. Lulu ran to the bow in order to ride like the queen with the wind blowing her white silky hair like a *Vogue* fashion model.

I walked to get to deeper water on the sharp rocks, praying not to get a gash on the bottom of my feet. This was to go on for almost the next mile. I kept getting in and out of the boat. The bottom of my feet were sore and cut from the rocks. The boat was filling with water as Baxter is like a huge bath towel, holding water only to drain it off in the bottom of the boat each time he got back in.

We finally made our way to the Connecticut River. Now we would surely make good time.

Or perhaps not! My exuberance was short-lived as we hit even more low spots. I looked at my map and checked my GPS. We would never make it to the island I had planned on camping on. I had not had time to find an alternate camping location before I left.

Looking at the map, I found a couple of smaller islands and decided to make my way there. We would just get going early in the morning to make up for lost time.

As we approached the island, I saw it was actually not much more than a sandbar in the middle of the river. It had some low reeds spreading out across its long narrow expanse. It was otherwise covered in small, jagged rocks.

My heart sank. I was exhausted, and a feeling of overwhelm set in. I began to realize I was not as prepared as I had thought. Once again, that cavalier spirit had caused me to continue without following the example of my father because "I wanted to do it right then and there." Can you picture a 55-year-old woman throwing a temper tantrum? Yup—I am embarrassed to say that was me!

There was no turning back now. I would have to make the best of it. I got out and walked the kayak toward the island, pulling it up onto the shore. The sun was going down, so I wanted to get our camp set up quickly. The dogs went exploring while I set up our home away from home. Putting the camp lights in the tent gave me some joy as I stood back looking at our little tent.

Holy tamole. We were going to sleep in that little thin fabric tent in the middle of the wilderness on the Connecticut River and not on the designated AMC campsite, where I had envisioned sitting around a campfire with other paddlers, comparing our stories. What the heck was I thinking?

The AMC campsite was said to have a bear box where I could keep our food for the next day. There was to be a wooden platform I could pitch my tent on. There was a fire pit to make a fire in, by which I would sit and have my nighttime tea while writing in my journal before heading off to sleep in peace. Sigh…

I dug out the food for the dogs and got them fed first. I pulled out my camp stove and decided to eat. Everything would look better after I had a warm meal of chili mac and cheese in my belly.

The sunset was beautiful, and it was very, very quiet! There were no trees to hang my food from on the island. I thought better of trying to wade across the river to hang it up in a tree on the eastern bank. So I resigned myself to the fact that we might not have any food left for tomorrow after I decided it was safer to put it about 50 feet upwind and away from the tent. Although it was early, we decided it was time to go to bed. Let me rephrase that. I decided it was time for bed. The dogs just follow my lead. After all, I am their pack leader.

We piled into the small tent made for one and tried to get comfortable on the rocks. This was going to be a LONG night. As I lay there listening to the dogs breathing, I listened for noises outside of the tent. As is the norm, everything sounds so enormous when you can't see it.

My imagination is very robust. I kept thinking bears would surely smell the dogs and not come near us. I left the food over there guys! Just leave us be! I drifted in and out of sleep for what felt like hours. I checked my phone. Nope, it had only been one hour. I decided to plug the phone into my portable charger and play my favorite worship music. Finally, I drifted off to a deep sleep, waking up a few times, but managing to shift carefully on the rocks and fall back to sleep.

I woke up at my usual time, 4:30 a.m. While I was a bit sore from the rocks I felt inspired. I got up and began to see the glow of sunrise. "This is going to be a glorious day," I announced to the pups. I went to see what was left of our rations and was pleasantly surprised to find it was ALL still there, intact. Thank God! (Side note: I have since invested in a bear canister.) After eating and packing up, we headed off. I walked the kayak down along the bank of the tiny island to get to deeper water.

I literally laughed and cried all at the same time as I discovered, at the end of the island, a beautiful sandy beach. Had I simply taken two minutes to investigate the island last night instead of just taking my lot in life and assuming I was meant to sleep on the rocks, I would have found this soft luxurious sand to have settled into for a peaceful sleep.

Sometimes life can be like this. We resign ourselves to a fate that WE deem to be our own when, if we took just a moment to look around, we often will find a less rocky place in which to rest, a path that is not so difficult.

This caused me to reflect back on the times in my life that were incredibly hard. I had been too worn out to be able to see a different way. I stayed on that rocky, uneven path where I kept stumbling, at times falling, getting bruised and scraped, sometimes even with deep gashes.

I see now there were other paths I could have taken that may have initially felt like going off into the wilderness for a bit. Ultimately, they would have gotten me on a smoother road sooner. This is not to say I am regretful. God is absolutely using all of it for good.

Growing up, when something did not go quite as I had planned, my father would sit me down and say, "So what did you learn from that experience?" In order to move forward, sometimes it is necessary to reflect back with that 20/20 vision in order to actually learn the lesson that was being taught. I have come to view trials as opportunities for growth and refinement.

Since this trip, I have applied the wisdom I took away to times when I find myself rushing or can only see the negative outcome. I pause, think back to that island, and decide to look past the rocky shore to see if, by some chance, a sandy beach can be found. I am pleased to say that more often than not, there is. And if by chance there is not, I also take comfort in knowing that one rough night sleep is not going to break me. The sun will come up in the morning to a bright new day.

Psalm 30:5b NIV

"Weeping may stay for the night, but rejoicing comes in the morning."

6
ROUGH SEAS AHEAD CAP'N

Day two of this adventure began with a gorgeous sunrise. Mystical fog hung over the river as we set out to complete 25 miles. The day was going to be full sun, in the 80s, and low humidity. I was feeling strong, bold, and confident despite two nights of restless sleep.

As the sun rose up above the mountains, the river was like glass. The picture on the cover of this book was taken at that very moment. If you look carefully in the distance of that picture, you will see a bend in the river. Hence the name of the book.

Just as in life, we never know what is just around the bend that we cannot see. I do not have any photos from the rest of that day, and there is a good reason for that! What lay around the bend this day was not at all what I expected.

Have you ever had a day that started out magnificent only to turn into mayhem shortly after putting your feet on the ground? Well, that is what happened on this day. It would prove to be the most harrowing experience I have had on the water to date. Remember in the previous chapter I mentioned that the paddler book I had gotten referenced increased motorized boats in this area?

At about mile 10 of the 25-mile day, my serene picturesque scene was disrupted by a speedboat towing a water skier. Cool! Another thing on my bucket list of things I want to try, I thought.

As I was dreaming of how I would be able to ski holding on with only one hand, a jet skier came almost straight at me. Yikes! The wake caused water to pour over the port side into the kayak as we bounced around like a bobber on a fishing line. Well, okay then! I decided I would have to stay closer to the bank. The wake dissipated and we continued on our way for about another half mile.

Then it was as if I hit rush hour traffic. I had boats of all sizes headed right for me. Quickly, the river became like the high seas, with up to two-foot waves at times.

Our little inflatable was being tossed all over the place. We were taking on water like crazy. The boat was getting heavier and heavier and harder to maneuver.

As the big sleeper cabins went by with partiers on board, I could hear the passengers say "Oh, what cute puppies!"

I had to attach Lulu to the boat with a line in case she bounced overboard. Baxter was laying flat across the bow, which I was eternally grateful for, because he was the weight I needed to keep us from flipping.

I had to pull out and drain the boat as well as take a mental and physical break every 45 minutes or so. The stress was real!

As the day went on, the partiers were getting sloppier and sloppier. I was convinced we were invisible to them. Seeing near-collisions and boats losing control and almost flipping over only added to my concern. I now had a migraine from the strain. In order to fight the waves I had to really dig deep at times lest we be pulled out into the middle of the river and the fray.

It was a delicate balance. However, I could not stay too close to the river bank either, since the breaking waves were nearly beaching us.

My arms ached, and my spirits were low as I succumbed to the choppy water. I spied a clearing along the bank where trees would provide a much-needed respite from the high afternoon sun. I paddled toward the welcoming spot.

Baxter could not get out of the kayak fast enough and get his paws on solid ground. Lulu perched on the bow and leapt onto the bank once I was close enough that she could safely make it to dry land.

I struggled to get myself out of the boat and drag the kayak partway up the bank. After carefully tying the kayak to a secure tree, I decided to take some ibuprofen, eat a late lunch, and take a nap. Maybe when I woke up the conditions would be better. In spite of the constant noise of motor boats and the sound of waves lapping up on the banks of the river, the dogs and I fell fast asleep.

I was awakened from my stupor by a huge wave that overtook the boat and soaked all three of us. I sighed and, I will admit, let a few choice words leave my lips. I had some decisions to make.

What I also failed to share with you earlier was that my outdated phone charger had not been doing its job. Now my phone, which was my lifeline, was down to 7%. Great! What else could go wrong?! I quickly texted my "land crew" my location and that I may not be able to communicate until I reached my car, but assured them there was no need to be concerned. I am not sure who I was trying to convince—them or me.

I then went to the GPS map to see how much further I had to complete this segment, and to memorize some of the bends in the river in case my phone died. I estimated I had about 5 more hours to go given the rate we were traveling. In normal conditions, with the wind at my back and fully loaded, I can get to 3 mph or a bit more. I normally plan for 2 mph with rest stops. I am not sure I was even doing ½ mph! I could get off the water by sunset, and there was a clear sky. The river was wide, so I would be able to continue paddling by moonlight, if need be.

My friend had thrown a line out to me offering to come pick us up. For a moment, in a puddle of tears, I almost texted back, accepting defeat. But then I heard my father's voice again. "You've got this. Don't give up. Take it slow and steady. Focus on your destination. Envision the marina at the yacht club. FEEL what it will feel like to put your feet on the boat ramp. Don't let the chaos around you distract you. If you give up now, you will forever doubt your inner strength."

So I did some mental calculations, assessed my water and food supply, and emptied the gallons of water from the boat again. I literally stood up tall, squared my shoulders, and said to my furry crew: "We have got this—we are NOT going to tap out and call for a ride—we WILL get to that boat launch." As only dogs can, their unconditional love and support were displayed in their excited running in circles and tail-wagging. That gave me the additional boost I needed. So off we went again.

This time I was paddling with purpose. With each stroke, I concentrated on making it the most efficient one I could. I kept my eyes fixed ahead. I had to cross the river twice due to currents and islands, each time praying for God's protection. Imagine a bicycle now in the middle of that rush hour traffic crossing four lanes of restless commuters, all jockeying for position, weaving in and out. Oh, and by the way, they are all coming from Thursday night happy hour!

We were tiny and low in the water compared to these cruisers. The jet skiers were behaving like motorcyclists who thread the needle between cars going 90 mph, but I did not give in to fear.

I would look over my shoulder, look for a gap in the crowds of watercraft, and turn our kayak perpendicular to the river bank, paddling with purpose. Then I would straighten as two boats went past us, on both the port and starboard sides, causing water to again enter on not one side but both sides.

I found myself laughing out loud at the ridiculousness of the situation. I reflected on the fact that I had not seen one other paddler all day! That is because I was the only idiot who did not know this was a foolish idea!

As the hours passed on, the fumes from the boats and the blazing full sun were taking their toll on us all.

Baxter must have been getting seasick in the bow. He made his way back to the back of the boat, all 85 pounds of him crawling over me to drape himself over the stern, dangling his paws off either side as they skimmed the water. He put his head up against my back. Lulu was sprawled across my dry bag, which I had moved to the center of the boat so she would not drown in the water collecting in the bottom. I felt like a bad dog mom, but I realized that they would have it no other way.

I continued to stay focused and paddle us to our destination. It was now sunset, and I knew I was getting close as all the boats were starting to circle around this one outlet where I remembered there was a public boat launch. This was three miles from where I needed to take out. I was close.

I marveled at the process all these boats that had been bustling along all day had to go through to get off the water. It looked like bees all coming back to the hive. The jet skiers, not wanting to wait in line, were getting their last kicks in, going back and forth in a very tight area, not looking ahead at all.

I saw them coming right at me while looking back to see where their friends were. I stayed focused ahead.

I had no other choice at this point. Three miles would take me about an hour and a half in these conditions, which meant I could not afford to pull off again. My arms were aching, my head was pounding, I thought I was going to toss my cookies, but somehow I felt determined, and laser-focused. I was going to finish!

At long last, I could see the yacht club off in the distance. For anyone who has paddled in a larger river, it is misleading how far away something is. When I see a bridge, I have learned that it is not 10 minutes away, even though it looks close. All the same, just the sheer vision of it made tears of joy and relief fill my eyes.

I noticed one smaller motorboat, piloted by a fisherman. He was watching me from a distance. He was staying within range but moving forward toward the yacht club. He would turn his boat around to check on me. I imagined he was like a coach, keeping an eye on the situation but not wanting to interfere unless safety became an issue.

He continued doing this all the way until I reached the far corner of the yacht club. By then, he had seen that I was crossing the river, as the boat launch was on the east bank (to the left).

It was as if he was satisfied that I was going to make it. I felt like that was what my dad would be doing. He would be there, but not take away the victory by coming to the rescue unless he could tell I needed help.

When I got close to the launch, both dogs hopped out and swam to shore. They were relieved to be on solid ground! I could barely stand when I got to the ramp myself from sheer exhaustion. I got all the gear, my boat, and my dogs loaded into the car.

I plugged my phone in and texted everyone that I was safely in the car heading home. I had over an hour to drive with a raging headache, but I had accomplished the biggest trip to date under extremely trying conditions.

I learned a lot about myself on that trip. I am stronger than I give myself credit for. I can endure pain and suffering and no longer allow it to take hold and interfere with my reaching my destination. I now know that trials are not something being done TO me but rather FOR me! I can endure great stress and it does not break me.

My conviction to accomplish this quest is stronger than ever.

I have since made changes to gear to lighten the load, and got a brand new mega electronics charger. I feel at one with my kayak now that I know it is stable and sturdy. I can bob and weave (quite literally) as plans and conditions change.

When you have hours on the water alone, there is plenty of time for reflection. There were decades of my life where I felt as ill-equipped as I did that day on the river.

Instead of digging deep and staying focused, all too many times I succumbed to the mayhem, taking on more and more "water" to the point where I could not paddle one more stroke. At times like that my go-to impulse was to retreat, curl up in the fetal position, and hope it would just go away. I missed out on a lot of life's fullness.

Through my deepening faith, knowing I wear the full armor of God, that I am truly seen, and truly loved, I now know that I can boldly make it through these most challenging times.

All of these lessons relate back to my life journey. The river is preparing me for what lies around each bend in the river, whether the waters are rough or smooth as glass.

Isaiah 43:2 NLT

"When you go through deep waters, I will be there with you. When you go through rivers of difficulty, you will not drown. When you walk through the fire of oppression, you will not be burned up; the flames will not consume you."

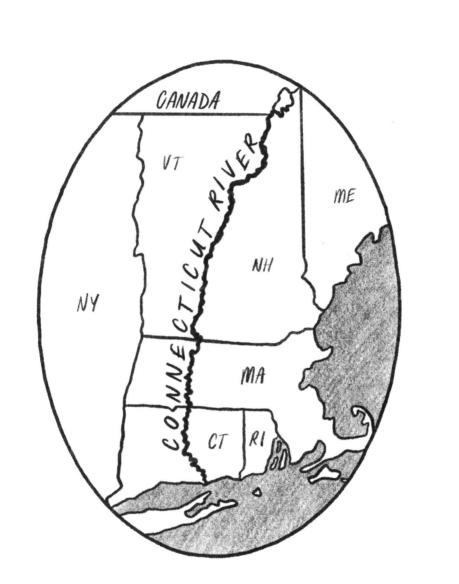

7

FORGIVENESS

FORGIVENESS! This word contains an incredible superpower. It does not come without immense effort, however. Lest you think my progress was achieved in a heartbeat, it has been an ongoing process for the past seven years and, to be honest, began initially in my early twenties. I have thought I had forgiven in the past, only to discover there was bitterness still remaining. At long last, I can say I have rid the last root of bitterness from deep in my spirit. My own story of forgiveness is a story of freedom leading to peace and joy I had never experienced before.

Until I truly understood God's grace I felt unworthy. My childhood dirty secret led to making ongoing, devastatingly poor choices about intimate relationships. The feeling of unworthiness permeated every aspect of my life. Friendships, lovers, and family relationships—all suffered because of it.

I felt worse and worse about myself. Dirtier and dirtier. I believed I could NEVER be washed clean. I worked, toiled, and worried each and every day to try and EARN back favor, to no avail. At one point, I even felt it was pointless, and went through a period of recklessness.

I finally got to the place where I felt like a smudge on the Earth, not even worthy enough to breathe air that could be used to fill the lungs of someone far more deserving.

It was on that day, after realizing my marriage was irretrievably broken, that I experienced a complete disassociation of spirit from my body. I remember it like it was yesterday, yet it was 7 years ago.

I was sitting at my desk at work. I felt as if I was splitting in two; not down the middle, but rather my body splitting away from my soul. I was taken over by an urgency to run. I had never in my life just up and left work with barely an explanation. It was as if I was on autopilot.

I was not intentionally controlling my actions. I fled to my car and drove directly home, got Baxter, and drove to one of our favorite hiking spots with a sharp cliff drop off at the peak. I had no conscious thoughts of what I was about to do. My body was moving me, not my mind.

I remember getting to the peak, and at that moment, I was hovering above, looking down on my physical body as it was standing at the edge.

There was no feeling at all. No color. No sadness. No pain. Just nothingness. I was like a piece of paper, standing on the edge of the ridge. A slight breeze could just blow me over the edge, and I would flutter down to the bottom of the cliff not to be missed.

All at once, it was as if my spirit reentered my body, and I felt a large gentle hand guide me back away from the edge of the cliff. I sat down and rested against a tree. I was dizzy and felt faint, but oddly at peace.

My mind was now back in control of my body and I realized I had responsibilities. I needed to pick my son up from crew practice! I somehow made it back down the trail, Baxter dutifully following along, and drove to the boathouse.

When we got there, I moved over to the passenger seat to let my son drive. I was still very out of it.

The crew coach and dear family friend came out to check on me. At this time, she was the only non-family member who knew anything about what was transpiring in our home life. She came to the passenger side door, took one look at me and knew something was terribly off. I got out of the car, fell into her arms, and I just remember her saying, "Breathe with me Jackie, follow my breath." I began sobbing uncontrollably. I realized right then what had transpired.

Through the grace of God, I was in my friend's embrace and not lying at the bottom of that cliff. I shared what had happened with my friend through my sobbing and gasping for air. Understandably, she was torn between bringing me to the hospital and letting me go home. She looked into my eyes and I earnestly said, "I am okay. I won't harm myself."

Weeks later, she would share with me that when she saw me that day, I was unrecognizable. "Don't ever scare me like that again!" I promised not to. Little did I know at that time, that was to be the first day of a brand-new life.

What transpired from there was God leading me through an intense journey of restoration.

I was introduced to the father of one of my son's crew teammates who "just happened" to be a pastor leading a home church. He and his wife welcomed me to their Sunday morning gatherings, where I sobbed through each message. With each tear shed, a bit of pain was being washed away.

I still held onto my secrets, as now I had even more.

While I have two beautiful sons, their father and I have been pregnant five times, with three pregnancies terminated. I lived in complete agony from this. In all honesty, this was far more devastating than anything else I had experienced. The day I shared this horrible truth with the pastor and his wife, I thought surely I would not be welcomed back. I had been hearing of God's grace, but I did not believe it applied to me.

As I shared with them my belief, they both had tears in their eyes. At the time I thought to myself, "See, even they know I am too far gone." It was not until after I went through a post-abortive healing program that I came to understand grace. It was there that I fell completely into the arms of Jesus and knew that He had not turned his back on me ever. It was I who had been running away.

I now understood that the pastor and his wife were not crying because I was too far gone, but rather that they ached for me. There were no words they could say to get through to me. I had to experience the healing power of grace for myself. I was able to now grieve the loss of my three unborn babies.

It is imperative to grieve in order to heal. I had been robbed of that process at the time having to face the anguish all alone; not feeling as though I even had the right to grieve. It was not to be discussed! At long last, if God could forgive me then I could forgive myself.

Continuing on that healing journey, I went through training to become a facilitator of the program and pay it forward. Watching other women enter the program, deeply wounded, and walking alongside them on their own healing journey, has filled me with incredible joy and only more deeply healed my own pain and forgiveness—both for myself and others.

Forgiving others, especially those who are no longer here or those who refuse to admit they have done any harm, is layered to say the least. I have gone through many levels of forgiveness each time thinking that was it, I have forgiven them, it is complete. Yikes! It is complex, and if anyone tells you it is simple, I daresay they perhaps have more work to do themselves. Or they are way better at understanding the concept of forgiveness from the get-go than me.

Over the years, I found myself in a place where I was living with an all-consuming anger, paralyzing pain, and isolating shame that was built up over decades and layers of "stuff." I have shared a lot in this book, but there is much more "stuff" which is irrelevant here. The immense root of bitterness that grew because of it is not.

I found myself spinning in an exhausting battle between wanting to hold on to my bitterness for the hurt and betrayal dealt me, thinking that forgiveness meant I was saying what happened was okay, and yet desiring to let it go.

It was only when I myself experienced His grace that I finally understood the redemptive power of forgiveness.

I am not pretending it is easy! No! It is excruciatingly difficult to let go of the anguish and move to a spirit of forgiveness. It requires the Spirit to be at work within you. Just when I thought I was "good" I uncovered new areas within me that needed to be healed through forgiveness to others as well as myself. Each layer that was revealed and released brought me one step closer to a truly joyful heart.

Loved ones, if you are finding yourself today with a root of bitterness and anger in your heart I pray you will seek to let go and forgive...for YOUR OWN inner peace.

Matthew 18:21 NIV

"'Lord, how many times shall I forgive my brother when he sins against me? Up to seven times?' Jesus answered, 'I tell you, not seven times, but seventy-seven times.'"

8
Fair Winds And Following Seas

I would like to leave you with some thoughts for consideration. Invest in yourself! When you are feeling empty, you need to just STOP. Realize you are worth the time, energy, and money required to heal. This is not merely an investment in yourself, but rather a gift to the world. You cannot live out the mission God has charged you with if you are not full first. You will have nothing to give anyone. Remember the adage "it is better to give than receive?" That is because in actuality the receiving is in the giving.

I have one last story from my life experiences to leave you with. As I mentioned early in this book, I found myself in a place of starting over from ground zero. This included financially starting over.

During COVID, my family faced a crippling crisis, causing me to put my business aside for a period of time, as my attention was needed elsewhere. During this time, I was volunteering each Sunday to prepare and serve lunch to those who relied on the city soup kitchen, because due to social distancing requirements, they could not be open. I remember looking into the eyes of those I served, and often they would be wet with tears, thanking us for all we did for them.

Of course, I thought I understood the feelings behind the words, but I soon discovered I really had no idea! Because I was not actively building my business, the income slowed to a trickle until one day, when I checked my bank account, I realized I did not have enough to buy groceries for my family.

I felt like I had been punched in the gut. The words "Your little business is going to fail," spoken to me before leaving my marital home, came thundering back to my mind. I felt defeated. The reality of the fact that I had to feed my family sobered me back to the moment.

I began searching online for a Connecticut Foodshare mobile food pantry location. For years, I had donated to this worthy cause, never, ever thinking I would find myself in need.

I found a nearby location. I read the directions of what to expect and how to be prepared when arriving at the site. I picked up my reusable shopping bags, told my sons I would be back in a while (too embarrassed to admit where I was off to), and drove to the location on the website.

I parked my car and walked apprehensively to where the line was forming. It was 15 minutes until pickup would start. I witnessed the familiar banter among the community family, just as it would occur with the Sunday lunch service in my own town.

Recognizing that I felt uncomfortable and was obviously new, I was welcomed into the conversation. I mostly listened, being filled with the love and concern they each held for one another.

They were FAMILY. And they had welcomed this wayward stranger into their home. I was grateful. The line began to move forward. I was graciously ushered along and given instructions on what to do.

When it was my turn, I held open my bag as each volunteer lovingly asked if I would like the item they were providing.

As my bag got heavier and more and more food was being collected, my heart overflowed with gratitude, and I broke down in tears.

I could barely speak the words "Thank you, bless you, you have no idea what this means to me and my family."

I returned to my car, gently placing the bountiful offering that filled the bag into the back seat. I fell into the driver's seat and wept. Tears of immense appreciation poured down my cheeks.

I returned home, brought the food into the kitchen, and felt the kindness bestowed on me as I slowly and deliberately put away each and every item with great care. My sons came in at that moment and I explained where I had been. We had a long embrace, as often is the case with those you love, no words were necessary.

The following Sunday, as I was again serving those who I have come to know and love in my community FAMILY, I looked deep into their eyes as I tenderly placed each item in their bag. I was overwhelmed by the emotion I felt.

It was as if I could actually feel their gratitude. I could recognize it as I had just experienced it for myself. It changed everything for me from that day on. I realized that being a receiver made me a better giver. Hence, as I said before, the receiving is IN the giving!

As you finish this final chapter, I hope you were able to take away even just one seed that you may plant, nurture, and grow. May peace be with you all your days.

May you experience the joyful life of a dog. Yes—I said a dog! Just envision how happy a dog is when he is loving you! His life is complete! He is never happier than greeting you at the door with his favorite toy. Their tail is wagging so hard you swear either it is going to fall off or they are going to dislocate something. The greeting is the same whether you have been gone for five hours or five days!

The chapter title, "Fair Winds and Following Seas" is my wish for you. It comes from a nautical expression. The phrase implies that a vessel will have good winds and not have to pound into the waves. Its origin is unknown, but for the last century, it has been offered as a blessing of good luck in departing on a new voyage in life.

May we meet around the bend in the river one day, with fair winds and following seas. I look forward to pulling out on shore and catching up around the campfire about all the adventures we have had.

— *Jackie, Baxter, and Lulu*

We invite you to follow us on Instagram as we continue our Connecticut River quest.

About the Author

Jacqueline A. Baldwin, FSCP®, CLTC® is a financial advisor. She believes in providing a comprehensive strategy to create and preserve quality of life as the centerpiece in her approach to financial planning.

In collaborating with families, adult children of aging parents, corporations, and individuals, Jackie takes a holistic approach that is about more than just obtaining insurance and investment products. She believes in listening to her clients, providing high-quality education and information, and then designing financial plans that incorporate their goals and dreams.

Jackie is an author and speaker. She regularly speaks to groups, including business owners as well as individuals. She brings to light important timely topics such as business succession planning and preparing for a solid financial future through retirement. Jackie also believes in paying it forward and is a trained facilitator for NAMI, as well as other support groups.

She resides in South Glastonbury, Connecticut. Jackie may be found serving her community through outreach programs, kayaking the Connecticut River with her faithful companions, Baxter and Lulu, and spending precious time with her two adult sons, Sam and Ben.

About the Illustrator

Kenni Zipf is mainly a ceramic artist but enjoys every medium. She graduated with her BFA in sculpture and ceramics from UConn in 2023. She loves illustrations, as well as sculpture, sewing, crocheting, printmaking, painting, woodworking, and more. Although much of her time is taken up by art, her family (and their dog Calvin, who is a good friend to Baxter and Lulu) is the most important thing to her. Outside of the arts, she enjoys reading, cooking, baking, and watching silly reality television, all of which are fun to do at the same time.

Made in the USA
Middletown, DE
06 September 2024